The Landfill of Discount Messiahs

C. Michael Minkoff, Jr.

Published by
The Nehemiah Foundation for Cultural Renewal, Inc.
Sugar Hill, Georgia

First Edition Nehemiah Foundation Press 2008

Copyright © 2008 by C. Michael Minkoff, Jr.

ISBN 978-0-6152-1633-1

All rights reserved

For information about permission to reproduce selections from this book, write to Permissions, The Nehemiah Foundation, 980 Riverside Road, Sugar Hill, GA 30518

A few of these poems in some form have appeared in *erato journal of arts & literature 2007 & 2008*, edited by Shawn Delgado, to whom I give thanks. These poems were *To A Young Southeastern American, Ink Blots, Chiseled, A Gnat: A Poem, Samson Was A Tool, An Ungrateful Faust,* and *The Landfill of Discount Messiahs*.

A Plea To The Second Generation and *Passover* appeared in *The Counsel of Chalcedon* (2007 Issue 6 and 2008 Issue 2 respectively), a publication of Chalcedon Presbyterian Church.

This book would not exist if it were not for these instruments of God's blessing to me:

My wife, Vanessa

My parents, Mike and Debbie

My teacher, Tom Lux

My collaborator, Derrick Otis

You will say that these are very small sins; and doubtless, like all young tempters, you are anxious to be able to report spectacular wickedness. But do remember…It does not matter how small the sins are provided that their cumulative effect is to edge the man away from the Light and out into the Nothing. Murder is no better than cards if cards can do the trick.

–Screwtape

Surely, just as waters boil up from a vast, full spring, so does an immense crowd of gods flow forth from the human mind, while each mind, by wandering about with too much license, wrongly invents this or that about God Himself.

–John Calvin

Contents

I.

Spare Me 5
The Landfill of Discount Messiahs 6
Chiseled 9
Man Who Bears The Burden 10
The Heretofore Missing Link
    Between Stone Soup And Primordial Ooze 12
The Broad Way 14
Ink Blots 15
The Monstrous Ransom 16
Incident At Club Kalua 17
Scavengers 18
He Had Almost Gotten Used
    To Not Having You Around 20
Choice-Cut 21
Making Up 22
Play-Aggressive 23
Left Ring Finger Nail 24

II.

He Feeds Himself Himself 29
Autistry 30
A Gnat: A Poem 31
The Tomcats & The Bees 32
Role Playing 34
To A Young Southeastern American:
    About Your Character 36

Revising The Future 37
Needless As The Desert.. 38
An Ungrateful Faust, Unsatisfied
    With Fame, Longs For Soul............................... 40
A Mature Poet... 42

III.

A Posteriori: The Confirmation Problem 45
Samson Was A Tool 46
David's Sons... 48
The City On A Grain Of Salt Before The Ocean........ 49
The End Summon Song.. 50
Noah Valiant Stout, 1 Year Old................................. 52
Lost Loss... 54
For My Dad... 56
Passover 58
Praying As A Child.. 60
A Plea To The Second Generation 64

Notes 68
Acknowledgements.. 74

The Landfill of Discount Messiahs

I.

Spare Me

that I may recover strength, before
I go hence, and be no more.
                              Psalm 39:13

If my mouth is a fountain
and my lips are its banks,
then my teeth are stones
worn smooth by words.

Sometimes the stones gnaw
the clay during drought;
I expect some children
will pull them all out

to pin down a sapling
as a roof for a fort
or to throw in a river
if it gives them some sport.

So the banks of the fountain
will surely erode
once it loses the dignity of its stones.
And maybe there won't even be a dry bed

or a memory of any of the words I've said.
There won't be a sign to let the sojourners know:
You might have quenched your thirst here
some years ago.

The Landfill of Discount Messiahs

operates the longest-running
continuous service "last-chance" mercantile
open-air barter market in the world.
In our illustrious history, the powers
that be have never forced us to recycle:
few of our patrons have left our lot with less
than they disposed of.
If there ever were such a thing
as the "invisible hand,"
we've employed it here at The Landfill.

But we must close our gates, alas,
to focus on our long-neglected dump
duties. But this is good news for you,
the consumer, since all our "last chance"
merchandise must and will go!

Get here early to enjoy the best
selection of high-quality second-hand goods
this side of Gehenna,
                including, but not limited to:

    Skeet machine pre-loaded
    with a lifetime supply of shot-glasses.
    Comes standard with shotgun
    to finish the job.

    Blow-up girl that blows self up,
    that is, explodes on contact—
    hours of harmless fun!

    Video library of James Joyce
    writing his books down word by word.
    Other authors available upon request.

    Heap of pure cocaine. (Obviously.)

    Self-Help Books, all instant classics, including
    How To Gain From Hitler's Fame,

Chicken Soup For The Left-Handed Vegan,
The Porpoise Driven Diet,
and *Metaphorically Actualized
Hyper-spatial Interpenetration For Dummies*.

Get your vinyl recordings of *The Pledge of Allegiance*,
The Communist Manifesto, and
The Final Solution. Narrated by FDR,
impersonator. Unlistenably
scratched by stoned turntablist.

Insolvency Specials
on Subject/Object, Science/Religion,
Nurture/Nature, The Other, and other
Half-full/ -empty arguments.
Diplomas available in Bar-graph Hopping,
Panhandling Life's Questions, and
Telling the Difference Between Columns
(comes with certificates in Smoke,
Infantry, Newspaper, and Corinthian).
Redemption value: 1/10 of a cent.
Restrictions may apply, and will persist.

Bust of Charles Darwin.

Bust of Marilyn Monroe.

Plastic tubes of wooden nickels,
Rockefeller dimes. Gift-wrapped
in ticker tape. (Financing available.)

Poetry and other Unnecessary Capitalizations.

Likeness of Elvis on baby-blue
velvet tapestry, arm outstretched,
reaching straight into your living room.
Other icons available on request.

Used Jesus candle (waxy head waned off,
sacred heart still glowing),
worn rosary beads, phylacteries, legs of newt

    in steaming cauldron (with dry ice),
    constellation playing cards,

    and other brass serpents.

And remember to get here early!
Any merchandise left on the lot
by the last day of sales
(along with anyone still
clinging to it) will be collected
into The Landfill and, in fine, hidden
under fresh earth.

Chiseled

Michelangelo left love-handles
when he removed what wasn't *David*.

But they didn't have lo-carb diets, lite salad dressing,
herbal metabolism enhancers, zero calorie
soft drinks, or olestra-fattened potato chips.
They didn't have thigh masters or blasters,
or programs to tone muscles you can neither
name nor use to drive
your wilderness ready SUV
to the beach to get skin cancer
looking at your next wife.

Against that bulbous building cover boy
whose vein-wriggling arm
is a waist bracelet
for the anorexic role model,
whoever stood for David
wouldn't stand a chance
in a showoff.

But
our steroid-rotten bones wouldn't hold
their weight with the 300 at Thermopylae—
our unhanded swords would stick
up from our armored wreckage
like rebar from crumbling concrete.

Man Who Bears The Burden

God made man upright,
but they have sought out many devices.
                              Ecclesiastes 7:29

The iron in the earth
and in our veins
makes red the clay that
crusts his knotful hands.

He has forearms like the ironsmith
tree, tendons tense
as crane's cables, lifting
with as much strength, but
more intimately—

the sweat from his chest's rough caress
makes mud of the dirt and dust as
he braces the boulder.

With every heavy step
his shoulder blades compress and quiver.

He sets the rock in the navel
of some granite's belly
and takes one hand away
to test the boulder's balance.
When it leans, he grapples, lifts,
replaces it where it won't
shift.

The second stone he selects, as unwieldy
as the first, he sets
on the first stone point on point. It turns
and, with a threshing sound, settles.

Onto this foundation,
the builder lowers a third stone
like a crown.

Then he rests.

I see a boy and I know
the builder sees him, too.
This boy, sour as sarcasm, he fells
that pillar with a finger—
a great accomplishment.

**The Heretofore Missing Link
Between Stone Soup And Primordial Ooze**

*For His invisible attributes…have been clearly perceived, ever since
the creation of the world, in the things that have been made. So they
are without excuse. For although they knew God, they did not honor
Him as God or give thanks, but they became futile in their thinking, and
their foolish hearts were darkened.*
Romans 1:20-21

Since the jumbled magnetic alphabet on my fridge
is genetically identical to *Paradise Lost*,
and the Periodic Table discerns no difference
between a heap of marble dust
and the *Venus de Milo*…

Since you share 98% of your DNA
with the Apes and 95%
with a banana
which, of course, contains all
the ingredients for the poop
your body will make of it…

Please join me in praising Milton
for transforming 26 letters
and various signs into
a masterpiece of English literature.
Please join me in fond remembrance
of Alexandros of Antioch (whoever he was)
for sculpting an ode to Aphrodite
we still find beguiling
though she be arm- and humor-less.

And let's have a warm round of applause
for your innards
which process countless comestibles
without your conscious command
but (generally) allow elimination
at your convenience.

All praise to Mother Nature who

without any middlemen (unlike
Mothers Sculp- and Litera-ture)
cooked every one of us up
from Primordial Soup
with no recipe
or ingredients but
existing conditions,
random chance, and
asymptotically reason-defying
blank check chunks of time.

And lastly, give yourselves a big hand
for needing no hands but your own
to organize all matters
into their current states
of self-indulgent, chaos-crowning
ingratitude.

The Broad Way

You were tired out by the length of your road,
Yet you did not say, 'It is hopeless.'
You found renewed strength,
Therefore you did not faint.

You saw the dashes and lines buried
below the windshield like credits
to a film—the ones to come
the least important
to the crowd.

You saw the man-planted pines
beside the road blur
or be resolved
into triangle rows.

To you the truth is like the sun
spots that trail your gaze
even when your eyes are closed.

It started raining in the night.
The runoff channels crept
across your windows, wept
like the willow.

To you the truth cries
Gloucester's tears
that never slide
from his ductless eyes.

To you the truth is a lie
yet to be discovered.
You washed your hands of it in a truck-stop sink.

Jesus answered, 'You say correctly that I am a king.
For this I have been born, and for this I have come—
to testify to the truth, everyone
who is of the truth hears My voice.'
Pilate said to Him, 'What is truth?'

Ink Blots

A window keeps blocking
a ponderous moth
whose reflection still
hovers wobbling
on its tattered-sail wings
veined like crumpled leaves.
It's beating the air
on the longing side
of an unbreachable display case;
should be happy to have a desire
untainted by having.

That moth tattoos its delicate dust
in cryptic splotches on the pane,
while I confess to the window,
blind and just,
who suspends these faint records
of relentless failure.

The Monstrous Ransom

The nurse-man says *So sorry*
as the needle pricks her hip,
the sting precedes a cold bruise
growing under her skin—
the most painful part of the trip
for her.
She is asleep

when they scrape out her womb,
and suck
the matter out through a tube.

She dreams its disassembled body
reforms on the Enterprise,
and Scotty gives the child
a medal for its self-sacrifice.

A girlfriend had come
to drive her home;
her boyfriend hadn't known.

They went straight to the mall,
she felt like shopping, her
girlfriend said there was nothing
stopping her now.

There was another child, years later,
with a different man.
She tries to be as un-
divided as she can.

Incident At Club Kalua

Today a 23 year old black man celebrating
his bachelor party was shot and killed by undercover
police officers outside a strip club
in New York. Over 50 shots were fired...—News

He was red-eyed and randy
when he stumbled from the strip club
smiling. He let his head fall
back and blew smoke
toward a street light.
His groomsmen helped him to his car
by his armpits. It was a quarter to 3.
They sat in the back;
he turned the key.

He heard the crash after,
the unmarked van too close
                    to his dashboard.
Then he felt the blows
in his shoulder and chest. His car
aerated by slugs and shrapnel.
He heard the tinkling
of brass—a noise you hear in movies.
A smoke usurped his nostrils,
seeped out his mouth
unexhaled.

When his fiancée heard the news, her hand
became mechanical,
a windshield wiper sweeping,
                            caressing
the swelling belly pitched
over his child.

Scavengers

You can't hear their paws.
They sound like dirt falling off cleats
into the grass.
They climb up the box fence
that almost hides your trash
from the neighbors.
They land with the softest kiss
on the lid over your refuse,
and pull the can down like
a child-laden sapling branch
that never recoils.

Your neighbor, the quiet one, just got shot
in the head by a burglar
in a dream. The gun fired when
        the can fell,
clanged, started scraping at the ground
vomiting—he feels his face
for blood.

Next morning, your neighbors can see
the bottles empty of beer, half-pregnant
with cigarette butts, pizza boxes gleaming
with grease constellations, well-fingered bathroom reading
(*TV Guide*, *People*, *Cosmopolitan*), the shrunken heads
of uneaten fruit, maggots in the Lo Mein, broken light bulbs, brown
paper bags (once wet crumpled now dry ancient looking), heels of
Wonder Bread like the cardboard but for the proud green velvet they
wear. Ashes, rot, curdle, and slime of every color (that is… brown) and
texture—slick as leather, lacquered like plastic, fuzzy like a Chia pet,
lumpy like cottage cheese, brittle as candle wax, nacreous as oil,
soft as decay…

Your daughter comes out in her sleepwear
(threadbare shorts and a translucent
t-shirt; no bra)
to get the mail at her usual time—
your neighbors know when.
It's cold outside.

Her eyes squint at the sunlight white on the
driveway. She leans over…
all the garbage.

The mother next door calls her boy
away from the window, puts her
celebrity magazine down.

It's not nice to stare,
she observes.

He Had Almost Gotten Used To Not Having You Around

He pulls the stopper behind the faucet;
water fills the sink. He flicks the surface
with his fingers—a flesh-colored dove
baptized in a birdbath, or drowning.

He wets his eyes for some relief,
the closest he'll come to crying.
He watches himself in the mirror—
in his pajamas, 3 p.m., shaving. He wonders

how they juice pomegranates. You appear
at the door in a suit. He cuts
himself—he hadn't heard you
come in the house. Your heels tick the tile

as little as possible. You slide
by him, get your hairdryer. You set
your key to his house down with a click. He hears
you louder down the hallway.

The front door closes. He shakes

out the razor in the sink—blood
spreads like cream in black coffee, pinks
the sud peaks peppered with his beard.

Choice-Cut

I know this vegan woman.
She once gave me this glossy-paged
pamphlet full of garish pictures.
There were cartoons of smiling pigs
disemboweled for their bellies;
cut in slabs and served for breakfast
to some red-faced caricatures.

There were beakless chickens covered
in their own feces, whose unused claws
had started growing into their legs.
And tongueless cows with clouded eyes
rolled back into brainless heads
which hung skinless from
hormone-deformed bodies. Then

there were alternatives: cute chicks
and talking broccoli lauded the health
benefits of an all-vegetable diet.
It was like an adventure ride at Disney World,
and the expected feel of relief at the end
almost convinced me to change
my eating habits.
Even if it is really inconvenient.

A couple weeks after, I showed her
some pictures—
photographs of partial-birth
abortions: babies half-way out of the womb
have their necks snipped, brains sucked
out of a rough "x" scalpelled onto the back
of their soft heads.

She slapped my face,
called me a bastard.

Making Up

When someone's phone voice
called us home,
I silenced the T.V. and tapped
the door like a good chaperone.
In the car, you put on
the album I had just heard
through his bedroom walls
to a slightly different tune.
In case Dad was awake,
you took care your hair
was fixed and lips stuck.
I was old enough not to ask
what was going on
behind all the making up.

Two months before I played
token groomsman, you sobbed
a public secret into my neck
with the restlessness that kept
you going. On the day,

you took your time down the aisle,
though the whole church could see
that your mascara was running
(only virgins wear veils),
and that you had two months more
showing.

Play-Aggressive

She used to be blind
almost. She knew me by smell;
she wanted to be held.

Now she bites me with her
felines, each one sharp
as a tongue-sculpted
candy cane.
She scars my arms
with her blackberry thorn claws.

I wish she would just
let me pet her
and purr.

Left Ring Finger Nail

On the sofa arms
to each side of the nail
the skin pulls off like string cheese
but it doesn't taper,
it gets meatier,
so you have to bite it off
(unless you have tools)
or you could keep
pulling into more pain.
Then there are loose tabs of keratin
you cannot resist, but regret,
correcting when pulling on one exposes
a frail-rippled ribbon barely
covering skin the red of light
in the womb.
And, of course, now
it must be even.
So you grind the thin oyster
rim blade pulling up skin and nail
together until the nail bed is half
as long as its neighbors
and looks brittle and layered
as mica.

You shouldn't chew your nails.
You look effeminate.
Your wife says it with her brow
wrinkles crimped at the point
where she doesn't wear a bindi.

You think through avenues of response:

there's the Sarcastic Playback—
with a soft tongue touching front teeth,
and jaws opening frown-fixed lips,
say *nihnuh nehnuh*.
Or the Defiant Revision—
You shouldn't talk. You sound like an idiot.
Or the Pathetic Defense with imbedded, though not subtle, barb—

One of us has to be the nervous, nurturing type.
And last, the Honest Question—
Why are you doing this?

But, instead, you put your hand
on your knee. You bite down
a little harder on the crescent
you just tore off with your teeth,
and you repeat the last line
of every dramatic romance film
wanting to reassure its mostly
divorced audience that everything
will work out anyway—

Okay.

II.

He Feeds Himself Himself

The poet is an eight-legged beast;
his many eyes reprise like an ancient wonder.
He sips from his prey what his fangs release,
the poet is an eight-legged beast.
He leaves the empty shell where its struggles ceased;
others see it suspended in his web and ponder
how the poet is an eight-legged beast;
his many eyes reprise like an ancient wonder.

Autistry

I saw two Mexicans
on some beige tile filling in
grout the color of fertile soil.
Each swath of wet mud from their
rectangle tools cleared its path
of the lines before it
(like marks on a whiteboard),
and dried unevenly in gray-scale thunderclouds.
The tiles glowed through where they could
and the un-squeegeed grid's
perfect square lines were
transgressing their boundaries
like ink bleed saturating the edge
of uncut paper.

I looked but saw no one
else around to share this vision
until a man walked up
to the safety tape.

They're filling in the grout, I said, excited.
He spoke to the men in Spanish.
I like the way that looks, I said, startled
by the urgency of my voice.
He kept speaking Spanish to his men.
He reached for the cell phone on his belt.
I realized
he probably thought I was retarded.

A Gnat: A Poem

He had wings like
                two pointless exclamation points
cut out of non-stick cellophane.

His abdomen and thorax together were like
                two periods as big as poppy seeds.
His legs were
                six minute apostrophes.

He was flying around my head in frantic spirals
whining.

He finally landed on my finger,
and I edited him with my thumb.

The Tomcats & The Bees

Carpenter bees (*xylocopa virginica*)
will chew perfect holes into wood—
holes that look like an over-eager handyman
decorated the side of your house
with a half-inch drill bit.
They will bore their bulky blackness
into your timbers all summer,
and then wait out the cold
in the recesses of your walls
until the warmth of Spring
draws them out again.

Last winter, we added onto our log cabin,
and what used to be the east side
exterior became a wall
in my bedroom. It was a cold January
and my wife set the thermostat to 71.
Some bees received a strange message
in their sleep, and soon,

too soon,

their unblinking black heads
were sprouting from our walls.
But they didn't know up from down.
They would fall out their holes
like an excess of dried plaster
and try to fly into the ground
as if it were the sky, tiring
out the wings pinning their backs to the floor.

Our cat got wise. He
waits at the holes
gurgling in anticipation as another bee
hits the wood just before
his paws come down.
If it had been any other kind of bee
it would have stung him,
but the carpenter bees that leave the brood

don't sting, so he flings
them at the walls and windows,
and bats them out of the air.
They try to escape by crawling,
but in their sluggish, almost drugged, state,
they never get any farther from danger
than he throws them for the thrill
of capturing them again.
He keeps chewing on their bodies
until they foam wet sawdust
and stop twitching.

Then he forgets they exist;
he curls up on a recliner and dreams
about the mountains of Cat Chow
he'll climb with his jaws.

Role Playing

So these people saw how you looked
with one ridged tooth
trying to force its way into your
stupid smile.
If they didn't pull your hair out
outright, they made you
wanna do it yourself.
They pulled your pants down
in front of the girl you all liked
to win her favor, and lost out to older boys
anyway.
These were your best friends.
They felt their first rush of power
calling you a dirty word they'd heard
on the receiving end. Older brothers
would also teach them how to punch
"you know where."
You would read the same books,
learn the same sourceless slang,
play with the opposite sex together.
Role-playing games—
starting with "house" and going even as far as
"relationship" somewhere in your senior year.
You would listen to whatever was clean
enough to get on the radio, but rebel enough to
make you feel older, or less vulnerable. You'd smoke
a cigarette to get another rush.
Another with that girl, I can't remember
her name. Eventually alcohol.
You'd stop counting maybe after alcohol.
You would spend
twelve years resisting maturity
together acting grown up, and then
nothing. None of the letters, calls,
e-mails, faxes you promised
in those summer vacation yearbook scribbles
as easy and resigned as suicide
                                  by falling.

And then, somehow, you meet again at the grocery store
out of state, in a different country even.
And you settle for a moment into the old
order of things. Maybe you shake the hand
a bit too firmly, or sulk just a bit recounting
all the evils you've endured for approval.
Joking, of course.
Sometimes, they seem very different. They have twelve children.
They moved to Salt Lake City, became Mormons.
Or you meet the bully, and your mom was right:
he really did turn out to be a loser. He hides
the forty of malt liquor he can't wait to taste
and extricates himself and his yellow-stained tee-shirt
from the humiliation of telling you
he actually is one of the people
who ends up careering at the corner quick-stop.

You both act like you imagine adults would
in your situation—
without visible envy. Forgiving. Interested.

What's new?

Nothing much. You?

To A Young Southeastern American: About Your Character

I saw the sun radical on the back of your car yesterday. You had politely translated it "Sun" for all those who did not read Chinese. The character was beside a yin-yang decal wreathed in flames as if it were itself…the sun. But the sun radical is not pronounced *yang* and it does not mean "sun." It means "day" or "date" and it is pronounced *rruh*. The character for "yang" requires an ear radical to the left of the sun radical. And "yang" represents the bright, overt, masculine side of the "yin-yang," so wreathing the whole symbol in flames is actually counter-meaningful to its balance. If you wanted to be accurate you should have left the "yin" side out and just had the white side and dot wreathed in flames. Though this would more aptly intend your specific brand of erudition and masculinity, it might still indicate that you are overcompensating for something.

P.S. I hope that you are not telling anyone that you are any one of the following: a Buddhist, an artist, or "moving to California." I am sure you are more than likely a waiter who thinks the OC is an accurate portrayal of California and your Buddhism has more to do with maddening your Baptist parents than following any perceivable moral conviction of your own.

Respectfully yours,

This Poem's Speaker (A Jerk Who Sees You Somewhat Clearly Because He Did Exactly What You Are Doing, Currently Regrets It, And Envies Your Bliss)

Revising The Future

Our memory *could* have a past and lack only a future,
but we don't read what our forefathers wrote or read.
We select some figures, and then we fit them to our culture—
our fathers are what we make them once they're dead.

But we don't read what our forefathers wrote or read
because we don't want to know if we believe a lie.
Our fathers are what we make them once they're dead,
and they make us in their image before we die.

Because we don't want to know if we believe a lie,
we design committees to agree on the truth,
and they make us in their image before we die;
we build them schools so they can also shape our youth.

We design committees to agree on the truth;
 they are guiltless. They just believe what they've read.
We build them schools so they can also shape our youth;
children have no reason to oppose how they're led.

They are guiltless. They just believe what they've read—
our fabricated heroes always do what they're told.
Children have no reason to oppose how they're led;
consequences always follow the ideas we hold.

Our fabricated heroes always do what they're told—
we select some figures, and then we fit them to our culture.
Consequences always follow the ideas we hold—
our memory could have a past and lack only a future.

Needless As The Desert

    Aug. 17, 2006. Concert.

I had turned the bottle down already
    (half-drunk, sweat-covered, pale-plastic)
once without a word—
held up my palm like a white-gloved cop,
and kept waving other traffic through.
My teeth were filmy, my eyes white only
behind the lids, but bloodshot as embarrassment
because of the dry lights that obscured the band.
My eardrums were being
shaken like aluminum flashing
that pretends to be thunder off-stage,
but too
    (early, late, loud, soft)
to help the audience
suspend their disbelief.

Robert Zimmerman was 'singing'
How does it feel? like it wasn't a question
anymore. He had re-arranged the melody
maybe
    so no one could sing along
or
    to mimic the moment the song was conceived in heat—
    but it was the miser fanning fading coals
    to get one last glimpse of his gold gleaming.

Almost before I made the choice, the bottle
touched my lips. Water
was absorbed into my throat
like gasoline into the air
from hot tarmac.
It had brought the filling
and the lacking both because
it knew I had to hear my pardon
to realize my crime.
One can choose to hate something
as presumptuous as forgiveness,

but I was grateful when it gave up
its last few drops, and I, the *complete unknown*,
gave my last three dollars
to those price-gouging vendors
for another bottle.

Meanwhile Robert Zimmerman was unfurling
his colors, less the chameleon and
more the peacock,
still croaking and cracking.
His voice
    as needless and beholden as the desert.

An Ungrateful Faust, Unsatisfied With Fame, Longs For Soul

I can tell by his blank goat grin and unswerving approach that this man is another demon come to torment me before my time by reciting his favorite line of my poetry. He has remembered this line by repeating it again again in his mind, the line muscling out every other thought—like the mental note to pick up a can of cranberry sauce on the way home. It is his mother-in-law's favorite part of Thanksgiving dinner, but he forgets this too until tomorrow when he is reminded of it again again by at least three different women, and by his son, who looks nothing like him, a fact I would cuckold him for if I wrote plays in the 16th century.

Yes, he has remembered this line with the desperate tenacity of an Alzheimer's patient, and I must be the benign mental warden while he relishes this line, this cursèd line, which I long to exile to the hamster wheel of his mind, but it has escaped my own grudging lips, and other more willing ones, already too often. So I receive it as any sane person would—like a remark about the weather you've already heard twenty times today from your senile grandmother who was raised in the South and thinks it polite to mention the rain to strangers, i.e. everyone, when she meets them for the first time, i.e. every time.

That line again again, that line that got you published in that famous journal; you have preserved it, at one time pungent as fresh pine needles, because of the same impulse that forced you to pick the skinny friendless kid for your kickball team. An impulse you wish to be rid of when the line, this line again again, performs like that skinny kid, planting his face somewhere between home and first, bleeding from his nose, and blaming you for making him play.

The ugly truth is that I hate most every line that's famed me. But without those lines, and the demons that come with them, I would have *never* gotten Big Name Press to pick up either my English verse translation of *The Wasteland* or that epic poem, too subtle for most, which insinuated the Latin names of toad species into rhymed couplets about the failure of the American Dream (an old theme, but freshly revisited, if I may flatter myself).

And I can't condone him, but I know what drove Roger Waters to spit in the closed eyes of an adoring fan singing along to *Animals*, if we can, I hope, assume Waters was *not* trying to heal the fan's perceived blindness with his Messianic spittle—an alternative interpretation that is somehow more repugnant. I know Beethoven wanted to hammer fan's heads to the time of his 5th symphony when its infectious intro kept turning over in their *Huhm Huhm Huhm* hums. Probably not, actually, since he was deaf at the time. Lucky him. And what about Poe? I am sure he did not die from alcohol poisoning or opiates or heartbreak or whatever. *Nevermore* killed him. *Nevermore* pushed his face down into a gutter and smothered him to death. And he was happy for the rest until he met that God-forsaken raven in hell. Still *quothing*.

And Shakespeare? Though I know I'm unworthy to even wipe the sweat off his ribald forehead, much less empathize with the man, I imagine how he must have hated *Romeo & Juliet*, especially when the court codpieces raved over it. How he must have written every tragedy after it as a penance, with every moment of comedic relief an attempt to drown its memory. Yet I am sure little *wherefore art thou*s still plagued his nightmares—rushing the stage and fawning him to pieces.

A Mature Poet

I have a glass of seawater
on my writing table—
which I sip. I'm done
trying to swallow the ocean
in every poem.
I have a heart staple
because my doctor said
I was *catharting* too much.
I try to make
my daily feel
satisfying.

I no longer write poems about
how I have nothing to say:
the constipation of the muse,
the limitation of language to express
speechless experience.

Aren't these mundane to one for whom
prune juice, senility, and accidental synesthesia
are daily trifles? I have already
written too much with my cigarette
and smoked too much with my pen.

I'm lying in the tub now; mashing
my lumpy skin into the cool porcelain;
dreading the cold dregs that still
linger in the showerhead above me.

My introduction before readings
is increasingly uniform.
It grows short.
It needs and will get
few further editions.
All of it can almost fit.

III.

A Posteriori: The Confirmation Problem

Houdini, master of escape,
once entered a *Harry Houdini
Look-Alike Contest*.
And came in third place.

The Pre-Modern Venetian State
regularly replaced aging
medieval historical art
with spatially realistic paintings
that their merchant historians would
then cite as more accurate sources
of objective history.
Apparently, their claims were less contested
when recorded in linear perspective.

Mark Dion replaced the fur
of a stuffed polar bear
with goat hair for his
installation *ursus maritimus*,
and it looks more real that way.

In other news, we have just
received a report of a missing person in
your community. The man's name
is Jesus of Nazareth. If you have seen
a thin-nosed white man
with chestnut shoulder-length hair
and a glowing disc of light
around his head, please
contact local police.

Samson Was A Tool

Say under the ruins of some temple
near wherever Gaza was,
they find Samson's remains—a shattered jawbone
sparse-studded with molars and incisors, two vertebra,
a couple fingers, and the bleached spade
of a scapula. The two soft tissues that troubled
his life and ultimately under-rubbled him
are, by this time, not even recesses
in his mouth and pelvis, both filled with sand.

The museum curator might paste his
brown-varnished leftovers in their respective places
on the black velvet wall of a display case
(like Lucy, the "first" human)
or, more likely, they fill his spaces with plaster
and wax and mount him next to a stuffed Saber-tooth.
Make him nine feet tall, gypsum femurs
thick as weaver's beams, his open mouth
battle-snarling, his dimensions aping
Goliath (a slight and unintentional irony).

Or wouldn't his actual bones be overlooked?
His Jewish features, unique among thousands
of Philistine corpses, have been scoured away:
skull clean of his contentious hair, skeleton
famished of sinew. We don't see Samson
onto this humble, even average, frame.
It's hard to imagine him blind and bound,
holding his shaking hands (calloused now

from the grain pestle rather than the spear) led by a child
to the pillars: beard uprooted, hearing only:
Where is your God, Samson? Samson, Where is your God?
They scorn the atrophied body that was never his
but now, more than ever, represents
Samson The Champion,
Judge Of The Jews.

But we don't see him.

In spite of all our posturing,
we prefer the M-16
to the ass's jaw,
and the plaster giant
to this shriveled grape
of a man.

David's Sons

The so-called king's speared side poured blood
but no water.

David's son hung above earth below heaven
while the soldiers clubbed
his majesty.
The once loyal people
hid their eyes
from his once flawless face.

Then
he could have passed for Jesus.

The City On A Grain Of Salt Before The Ocean

Between the gurgle and *shhhh* of one ocean tide,
tiny generations live and die.

As a wave recedes,
let the prophet rise:

Woe to you, proud doubters,
who cast the universe in your own shadow!
You should name your houses, 'Driftwood,'
and your city, call it 'Reef,'
your children's weeping is over-wet
by the ocean's Father's grief.

Though he may be derided
by experts in every field,
let the prophet not be silenced
by the trends that science yields:

The sampled sands have spoken—
No sea has touched this shore.
So we are sure none ever will,
Nor ever has before.

A short time proves the prophet wrong
in the grain-dwellers eyes,
and the doubters drive him inland,
but let his voice still cry
in the wilderness.

Let the wave also be still
like an hourglass on its side
because a day is like a thousand years,
a thousand years can pass in the night.

There once was merry-making,
marrying, and giving in marriage

before the ocean.

The End Summon Song

Irrational one, you negative root—
you unfocused insatiable *i*;
you balked at complexity,
put self over God, and limited truth
to that lie.

The Jackal convinced you in the beginning
that slavery would free you from ignorant bliss,
and the lie that begat your unsavory condition
is all you can hold to console
all you miss.

That barnacle guilt, such a clinging
crustacean, gives you no hope to come
because of what's passed.
You pendulum swinging,
you surf in a sea storm, you're holding
too quickly what seldom holds fast.

What's to hate about freedom?
What's so ugly in Hosanna?
Is it hard to trust Jesus the all in all?

*I murder my children
and opt for Barabbas,
I know about freedom of choice.*

It is gall
that you swallow, Gehenna
you live in. You got
pyrite and zirconium for The Pearl
you sold.
You know nothing of freedom
while your sin saps and bleeds you,
you rename the hand that feeds you
common sense, luck, power, gold.

*But I will not sing Hosanna— it is far too easy.
I want the credit due me;*

his burden is too *light.*
And science indicates that nothing is
so black and white.

Today's science is tomorrow's alchemy,
the future is some other future's yesternight—
a rotten tooth with which to chew,
a law for too many from too few,
a sound-byte all recite on cue,
a moldy song they gave in lieu
of the perfect fresh renewing truth.

But… Jesus? Are you jesting?
What ignorance you put to rhymes.
Should we be so backwards? How
can you be so far behind the times?

I could tell you of His glory,
I could stretch my tongue to frame
the advance of the Old Story—
still progressing
still the same.

I could prove that God still rules
us, though you trade His truth
for chains,
but your weighing scales still blind your eyes.
Your ears are stoppered with shame.

Turn, you wayward,
from the gutter water and famine food.
Return. Return to the One who made you—
Oh, taste and see that the LORD is good.

Noah Valiant Stout, 1 Year Old

Though He slay me,
yet will I trust in Him…
                    Job 13:14

Within a corroded chortle
like the startling mower,
I heard a familiar voice—
the voice that warbled through
the warm water in my mother's womb.
My first lullabies were
its low vibrations responding
to her higher pitch,
and I heard it in quick bursts
that would set my world heaving
with laughter.
Before I ever saw his face,
I knew my father's voice.
My eyes, full of blurry light,
darted to find him
in the crisp laden words
he spoke into the cold air
after my birth.

But my father's face is altered now.
Its holes are larger and the largest one
spews out black and red sound
to the ear what soap is to the eyes.
And his elbows lift and his arms bend
far above me like the branches
that hold tire swings.

I have seen my father lift
my mother off the ground
to kiss her.
He has held me and my brother
with one arm.
Whose arms are stronger than his,
and who could I run to for safety?
I bow my head,

too afraid to look at his gaping face.
I reach out and run
toward the voice that I trust,
though its roar is all that I fear.

Lost Loss

They say that all poetry
is about love or death.

I wanted to tell a story—
something he did everyday
that changed my life
now that he's dead.
I would recount it in a far-off
tone so the reader would know
how immanent the memory is
to me, how transcendent
(wishful thinking)
to you.

Or I could collect my grandfather's last words
as a synecdoche for his life.
But the last ones I heard were,
I want to get off this.
He was poking the mattress.

I said, *You can't get off
the bed; why do you want to
get off the bed?*

I wanna get off this. ...Process.

He pulled out the O_2 line
from his nostrils.

It was just to scratch an itch in his moustache.
He re-inserted the tube and wrapped
the line around his ear in a practiced
manner—like a book-keeper with his
ear-stowed stubby pencil or
a professor with the round arms
of his gold-rimmed glasses.

You could read in his obit,
which he wrote, that he had over 200

brass unicorn figurines,
and that he liked to visit
covered bridges in New England,
his childhood stomping ground.

But I know, because I was there,
that he was gasping in the very
end. His mouth stayed
open, a perfect wedge
of space between his
chapped straight-line lips—
lips like a fish have. Not for smiling.
Not for framing words. But sucking
air that couldn't make his blood
redder, his face graying.

I wanted to cry.
How expected, they say.
How banal. And I dry up.

But a poet,
this person, who strives
to expose the originary,
I have had my grief already.
Already prefigured, stolen, by so
many permutations of love
and death that
my loss is lost
in Frost and "Thanatopsis."

But my grandfather, generous,
had a subtle sense of humor—
he died on February 14, 2007.

For My Dad

Sundays Dad woke late; already suited
when we came downstairs
still trying our morning legs.
He made the best scrambled eggs.

It was late for him, anyway.
He graduated college with a wife,
and took the only job offer he had.
Thirty-four years. Five girls and one boy.
Thirty-four years. Same wife. Same employer.

Some growing up Saturdays
he'd take me with him
to his austere and lonely office
that he opened before dawn. He would put me
in a conference room in a too big recliner
with plastic rulers and paper for my round square designs.

Saturday was a short day.
He would take me to his barber Barbara,
the same woman who had given his hair
such conformity for so many years.
She would cut my hair
the two ways possible: buzz or trim.
And she would say I looked a lot like him.

After I failed out of college,
lost a few jobs,
sang a few songs,
and did what all the desperate people do
a few times at least, I moved
to California, *Other side of the continent*,
my mom said. That is when/where my sister called
barely choking out, *He's in the hos-spitt-uhl*.

My dad got better once my mom got back.
He had told her to stay in Florida
to finish redecorating their beach house.
Not one of us believed my dad would die

or even could;
so she took her time getting back, and I
lost another job waiting for my sister's hushed
phone calls. I filled out applications waiting in Carmel.
I had another job before my dad was well.

I moved back to Georgia with my wife.
Winter last year we drove over thirty-four hours straight through.
If you'd told me what that meant all at once in my old car
(driver side window didn't roll up so my face got chapped,
wife and I switching sleep in a passenger seat cramp)
I would have told you I wouldn't, couldn't do it,
but we didn't know what it would take, so we kept going.
My dad's moving into the house he'll probably die in.
I'm helping move his furniture on my Saturdays;
He keeps saying, *I'm tired, son.*
I understand what that means.

Passover

I think it makes sense mint jelly goes with lamb—
it means the Passover meal had the clean taste of forgiveness.
Now the Preacher breaks the bread and takes the wine
in his hand. It took me years to believe;
still I barely understand—how Christ makes an appearance.
Some things are hard to forget, some to remember.

In the Passover, God promised not to remember
the sins of any man who painted the blood of a lamb
on his doorposts. The Angel of Death, in the appearance
of a black cloud, passed over that house whose forgiveness,
freely offered to anyone who would believe,
gleamed in the night the color of red wine.

And now the Preacher again takes the bread and the wine
and has us all eat and drink, he says, to remember.
St. Augustine said, *I believe
in order to understand*, but as they sing *Worthy Is The Lamb*,
I think how it is hard to believe that forgiveness
would come having such a lowly appearance.

But I know, my father taught me, not to judge by appearance
so the next week as I sip the plastic thimble-full of wine,
I try to believe it is the blood of forgiveness.
But if God is not going to remember
my sins against *me*, why does He remember them against a lamb,
or gentle Christ, in this poor thimble, so hard to believe.

It seems easier for my grandmother to believe.
She has a thick black wig with the appearance
of real hair, but that it doesn't budge. She used to sing *...liddle lamb
zeadivy, a kiddle eadivy too, wouldn't you?* Maybe. But drink the wine?
It's not about the wine. We remember that God doesn't remember.
Countless lambs, bulls die pointing to Jesus—the price of forgiveness.

And when I think about the price of forgiveness,
I think of the cost of my weekly unwillingness to believe.
I had forgotten most of my life, but now I remember
how my sins, which in the movies have an innocent appearance,

broke Christ's body and poured out his blood the color of red wine,
and I think it makes sense mint jelly goes with lamb.

Because the Lamb whose blood was spilled
to grant the cleanness of forgiveness
is present, I believe, in the bread and wine.
And I will see Him some day in His glorious appearance,
but for now I will remember Him with my mind.

Praying As A Child

–for Evelyn Green

First I gave attention
to my black corduroy pants
with their subtle pied piping.
I could write my name
against the grain and sweep
it away with my hand
darker and lighter.

One can get bored sitting
as a youth and still.

Then the carpet, being also like suede, caught me
with its minute recounting—
the heavy steps I traced around
the loveseat and coffee table
abruptly cut off

at the brick hearth.
The vacuum lined uniformity
in the less traveled path belied
the almost archaeological complexity
of tracks covering tracks
in the common area.

The disheveled shag looked like the screen
of a broken Etch-a-Sketch,
or, if not broken, then rarely shaken.

If still bored, but more daring,
I would look up
like a possum reviving from its ruse,
gaining confidence with silence,
and finally moving about freely

with my eyes.
The low light glowed from the lamp
behind his head. His head that tilted.

His shoulders raised near his ears,
and his legs stiff-balanced on his heels.
His lips were barely moving.
He looked earnest and autistic.
His wife clutched her hands.
Her veins and vellum skin collected
like frail gloves
over her bones.

A chair squeaked settling so
I put my eyes down again.

My body was too taut,
not moved
in too long. I moved my pointed
elbows onto my knees and pulled
my feet like weeds, planting them
closer to the chair.
This revealed my own marks
on the floor's topography.

It reminded me of when I used
to overturn rocks in the creek.
I would pick one out,
sun-dusty and covered with dried moss,
and get two holds
on the small side of its ungainliness,
and strain with all the tenacity
of weekend yard work,
huffing like a tractor
as my muscles constricted
and the boulder budged, lifted,
and quenched its dust in the creek.

I wished I had not moved
my feet.

I closed my eyes
to listen, but I could not
keep them shut. I kept looking
at my soles' imprints on the floor

knowing they were the same as before.

I shoved my first knuckles
into the cool dough of my closed eye's sockets.
The small space between the lids
gave slightly and hot-moistened
my index fingers,
and I listened in the
maroon silence
of the bleeding light.

She was praying.

When I was even younger
she brought me books
suitable to my age—
about the caterpillar that ate too much
and even ate holes in the book you were
holding but became
a butterfly
when you least expected. Although,
you expected something
because you could feel the book's thin
"what's left" in your right hand;
that meant the end was coming soon,
and something always happens
at the end.

She is a hundred or so now.
Her praying voice is the unsteady arm
on the bladder of a bagpipe pumping
hard what's blowing too softly.
Arthritis shrinks her comfort
with each breath that breaks
her to draw. She lets in
spurts of air faster
than she can finish single words
which she draws over the in
and exhale
of that staggering volume
with a rhythm as consistent

and disconnected
as the wind chimes near the ocean.
You can hear her head bobbing gently
between words—

Fa-uh-thuh-herrr... wee-hee beh-see-heech... yoo-hoohh.

A Plea To The Second Generation

*So it came about when Moses held his hand up, that Israel prevailed,
and when he let his hand down, Amalek prevailed.
But Moses' hands were heavy.*
                      Exodus 17:11f

The war isn't over when the old soldiers die;
it doesn't expire with the day.
When the righteous hands are heavy, who will help hold them high?

Where is the herald to wring the air out with his cry
when the voices of martyrs decay?
The war isn't over when the old soldiers die.

Moses smashed the tablets at the foot of Sinai;
he unburdened his own hands in dismay.
When the righteous hands are heavy, who will help hold them high?

The second generation always makes the first one sigh
because they sit down to eat and rise up only to play.
The war isn't over when the old soldiers die.

Near Rephidim, Israel would have lost the fight
but Aaron and Hur bore Moses' weight.
When the righteous hands are heavy, who will help hold them high?

Our fathers are joining the witnesses in the sky,
and the broken line needs filling in their place.
The war isn't over when the old soldiers die.
When the righteous hands are heavy, who will help hold them high?

Dear Patient Reader,

Thank you for taking the time to read my book.
                    –MM

Notes

1. Apology

In some ways there are no persona poems, and in other ways, all poems are persona poems. I hope the reader makes a separation between the speakers of the poems and the poet. I have never published any poems in any famous journals, I have never met an old schoolmate out of town nor do I know any that have become Mormons, the cat in *The Tomcats & The Bees* was actually female, etc. Poems come from many different experiences, real and imagined. And they have many perspectives, real and imagined. I only say this because I find many of my poems have some rather despicable speakers. I see those speakers in myself unfortunately, but I do not wish to be characterized as any one of them. I hope the reader understands, and doesn't condemn my rather weak attempt to exonerate my character of the characters my character has produced. Thankfully, God's grace is sufficient.

I also wanted to mention, for the sake of some of my more squeamish Christian readers, my reasoning for including sometimes controversial or unattractive things in my poems. For instance, some Christian readers have been made uncomfortable by the poem *Scavengers* and others take umbrage at certain elements of *The Landfill*, etc. The question of balance comes into play concerning these things. When Paul writes "Do not even mention the deeds done in darkness…" he does not stop there. He goes on to say, "…but rather expose them." Given this need for the exposing of sin, I can make a case that I have not glorified or relished the sins I have depicted in my poems, but have tried to show them in all of their relationship-destroying corruption without overstepping the boundary-marker called *obscene* (which literally means *off-stage*).

It is also curious to me that modern Christians are more squeamish about sexual sins than they are about any other sins. They are also more squeamish when exposing sins than God was through his prophets and apostles. The Old Testament has many graphic and explicit sexual images as well as graphic descriptions of violence. A few passages for your consideration (though there are many throughout the Scriptures) would be Job 31:9-10, Ezekiel 23:20, the whole of Song and Solomon, etc. My Pastor has said that if we understood the idioms that Solomon employed, we would sell Song of Solomon in a brown paper bag. Obviously this is a slight exaggeration, but only a slight one.

Understand that the translators in many cases are not translating verses as explicitly as they may be written in the original tongue. Many know the passage from Isaiah 64:6 translated in the NIV as "When we display our righteous deeds, / they are nothing but filthy rags." This may be an adequate translation (the NASB says "filthy garment"), but it is not literally what Isaiah wrote. He wrote that our righteousness is like a used menstrual rag. In modern parlance, our righteousness is a used tampon in the sight of God. This is gross and disgusting and should make us feel uncomfortable. But it is nonetheless the Word of God.

Now I am not God, so it is possible that I have been graphic when it was not appropriate or been graphic in a way that was not appropriate, but I have attempted to expose my generation's sins so as to grip the hearts and minds of its people (as God gives utterance to me and a path of acceptance in them). I have attempted to follow the lead of the prophets for my method in this. I pray the reader will forgive me if I have perhaps gone too far, but I also pray that the reader will solemnly consider whether we as Christians have become "salt that has lost its flavor." In a culture as wicked as ours is, we could all use a bit more hard-hitting saltiness—a saltiness constrained, of course, by the light of God's Word.

2. Various and Sundry

Preface quotes from *The Screwtape Letters*, by C. S. Lewis, and *Institutes of the Christian Religion*, by John Calvin.

Quotations from the Bible are variously from the New American Standard Version, the English Standard Version, and the Authorized (King James) Version. Where possible I used the literal Hebrew translation. For the versions mentioned above not in the public domain, I include now the necessary copyright information:

Scripture quotations not from the KJV or ESV are from the *New American Standard Bible*, © 1960, 1962, 1963, 1968, 1971, 1972, 1973, 1975, and 1977 by The Lockman Foundation, and are used with permission.

Scripture quotations not from the NASV or KJV are from the *English Standard Version*, © 2001 by Crossway Bibles, a publishing ministry of Good News Publishers. Used by permission. All rights reserved.

Scripture quotations from the KJV are, I'm thankful, in the public domain.

Throughout the book, I put text quoted inside poems in quotation marks, all spoken words in poems in italics, and all epigraphs in italics. I may not need to explain myself, but I generally dislike quotation marks for poetry. I find them clunky and awkward to use, and they alter the look of a poem's line alignment.

3. On the Poems

Stone Soup is an old fable where a foodless hag tricks her neighbors into supplying her with food by telling them that she will make soup using nothing but water, stones, and magic. She tastes the soup periodically and says "It is very good, but it will need some [insert food here] to really be at its most delicious." In this way, she gets all of her neighbor's food while they marvel in the end and praise her for making soup "magically" without any ingredients. In this poem I also use the word "asymptotically." This word basically means "converging to infinity" for my purposes here. An asymptotic line is a line that converges to infinity on one axis while approaching but never reaching a certain finite value in a corresponding axis.

The first four lines of *The Broad Way* are from Isaiah 57:10 and the last lines are from John 18:37, 38. I did not reference them in the poem because they are lines in the poem rather than epigraphs, but I put them in italics to distinguish them from my own words.

The Monstrous Ransom is based on an actual case which I read on the website I'm Not Sorry (www.imnotsorry.net). This website is dedicated to women sharing positive abortion experiences. I think it is a very disturbing psychological smokescreen and encourage those of you with strong stomachs to read some of the stories. The title of the poem is a label of an old narrative framework where a woman gives up her chastity and her body to an evil man for the sake of something that the evil man has in hostage (this hostage is supposed to be something of greater value than the woman's purity, often a brother or one true love, etc.). This is an ironic title since the woman gives her body over to a worthless man for nothing and kills the loved one she should have been protecting with every effort. What was held in ransom was the higher principle of convenience, but it required the body of another to set that hostage free. How easy it is to give up the body of another for one's own sake. In this way, the unborn child becomes the pure woman of the narrative having its body taken by evil men to allow convenience to live. To me, there is a grave and terrifying ridiculousness to this scenario.

He Had Almost Gotten Used... was a homework assignment I did for Tom Lux. It required that I use "pajamas" and "birdbath" in a twenty line poem with no being verbs or passive tense, only two or three adjectives, and no adverbs.

He Feeds Himself Himself is a triolét.

Revising The Future is a pantoum.

Robert Zimmerman is Bob Dylan's real name.

Roger Waters is the singer for the band *Pink Floyd*. Poe did die face down in a gutter. Many people walked by his body, though none stopped to help him. It has been said, though it may not be true, that he drowned in about two inches of gutter water.

A posteriori, as opposed to *a priori*, is a form of reasoning based on induction and confirmation of hypotheses through experiment. *A priori* is argumentation based solely on reason, and requiring no outside information for confirmation. For instance, if I said that the sky was blue, one would have to look at the sky to confirm. One could not reason it out without outside information. This issue is brilliantly delineated in a recent book called *The Black Swan*, by Nassim Taleb. The titular argument involves the confirmation problem. For years, philosophers thought that saying "All swans are white" was about as pedestrian as saying "All bachelors are unmarried." Not until England colonized Australia did they find black swans. The point is that it is easy and misleading to rest your hopes on the confirmation of what you already believe to be the case, but confirmatory evidence of a synthetic claim means almost nothing since it only takes one contradiction to debunk a synthetic claim, even if such a claim has been confirmed for a thousand years. According to Taleb, every confirmation makes it even more dangerous, since it is trusted with more abandon and constructs more and more of our perspective on reality. The poem is about the fact that evidence is interpreted, therefore no evidence is objective. It is as if we all have different colored glasses when it comes to seeing the world. You say the sky is green, I say it is grey, etc. This is not a corroboration of ultimate philosophical or moral relativity as much as it is a statement of man's inability to know anything for certain from only his finite perspective. Though we all may wear glasses, God does not. There *is* an objective reality and an objective truth, even if we will never see it perfectly in this life through our finite and corrupted eyes. This is *precisely* why the Christian must "walk by faith, and not by sight."

For My Dad owes a great deal of its language and ethos to *Those Winter Sundays* by Robert Hayden.

Passover is a sestina.

A Plea To The Second Generation is a villanelle.

4. A Note About The Cover

The cover is not entirely surrealistic, though it does have an element of distortion (one could even say corruption). This is the junk-heap that is all our accumulated idols. It is, in fact, an awful place, but it is exactly where the ungodly want to be. There is no escaping this: the unbeliever chooses hell. Now, many an unbeliever has told me that *I* am unjust and cruel for saying *anyone* will go to hell, but I usually respond in this way:

Having never relished the church or worship here on earth, would you like to go to an eternal worship service once you die? Would you not rather go to a place where you get to do whatever you want and you don't have any responsibilities and you don't have to deal with the church or worshipping God?

Some would say that it is not an either/or situation, but it is. And I am not choosing the eternal destiny of any man. Each man chooses for himself when he decides to forsake or to cling to those things that God will most assuredly and unchangeably condemn to hell.

Hell, in English, has the same root as *hole* and *hull*. Our word *occult* comes from the Latin *occulare*, which means *to cover* or *to hide*. The whole purpose of hell, as indicated by the Septuagint's word *Gehenna* (which was the trash pit outside the gates of Jerusalem where refuse was collected), is *to cover* that which is repugnant to God. Hell is a landfill for idols and idolaters. So:

The light-posts of the landfill are gallows, since the wise of this world have their minds darkened, and since, as Hegel correctly stated, all merely human philosophies are *Philosophies of Death.*

Out of the pile of smut, sex objects, filthy lucre, and idolatrous drug addictions comes a conveyor belt of babies on their way to being sacrificed to the god Moloch (*Molech* in the Old Testament). Molech was a Sumerian god to whom children were sacrificed. The Molech of today is Convenience, to whom millions of born and unborn children are sacrificed around the world every year with the same passionless efficiency with which we manufacture consumer goods.

Poe's face is in the mirror that has become his guillotine, since the wages of the wicked (fame, money, pleasures, etc.) are treacherous.

Hollywood has become the Mecca of our godless generation (hence *Holywood*).

The television has replaced literature (Shakespeare) for a godless generation whose attention couldn't span a crack in the pavement.

And there are those who cling to literature and high aesthetics as well, thinking that the refinement of their idols will spare them judgment in that Day, but it won't.

And, of course, there is Darwin, the titular figure of that odious *ism* which has so stolen the hearts and minds of countless people who have darkened their counsel with ignorant words, unable to recognize through faith, though condemned by the clear record of Creation, that this world was not made by anything that is visible, but was made by the Word of God's power. They desire to be as gods (Darwin's arm is the arm of Michelangelo's God, not Adam) and yet have demoted themselves to the image of apes (*whose god is their appetites*), choosing oblivion, meaninglessness and absurdity over the dignity of service in Christ's kingdom.

Acknowledgements

Cover concept by Derrick Otis and Michael Minkoff with following exceptions:

>Vanessa Minkoff suggested a winding rather than straight path through The Landfill.

>Colleen Minkoff accidentally discovered the play on words "Holywood."

All Drawings and Illustrations by Derrick Otis.

Colorizing of Derrick's drawings (including the Warhol-ization of Darwin) by Michael Minkoff. Thanks, *Photoshop*.

This book in your hands paid for by Mike Minkoff, Sr.

Warm beds provided by Mike Minkoff, Sr.

Warmth in Michael Minkoff's bed, acrylic painting for cover, and good advice provided by Vanessa Minkoff.

Warm meals provided by Debbie Minkoff.

The Tomcats & The Bees and *Play-Aggressive* in loving memory of Ke'ai the Cat who was callously run over by one of many really bad drivers on Riverside Road.

Special thanks to Derrick Otis for burying Ke'ai the Cat.

Travis Denton gave me the idea for Elvis on blue velvet in *The Landfill*. In fact, I stole his words almost verbatim (with his permission, of course).

Tom Lux helped me to realize the importance of poetry that makes sense. He is the only and best teacher of poetry I have ever had. (Though as the only teacher, he is also the worst.)

www.ingramcontent.com/pod-product-compliance
Lightning Source LLC
Chambersburg PA
CBHW051712040426
42446CB00008B/843